Kites
Shapes in the Sky

By Catherine A. Welch

CELEBRATION PRESS
Pearson Learning Group

Contents

Shapes and Sizes

Do you want to learn about shapes and angles? Then go fly a kite! Kites come in many shapes and sizes. Kites can be made of triangles, squares, diamonds, and circles. Kites can have more than one shape, too. Some kites are small. Others are as a big as a barn.

In this book, you'll see kites made of many shapes. You'll also learn how they fly.

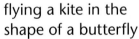

flying a kite in the shape of a butterfly

How Kites Fly

A kite weighs more than air. It needs wind to lift its **sail**. The sail is the paper or cloth cover. In light wind, a kite must catch a lot of wind in order to fly. The person holding the string flies the kite at a higher angle.

In strong wind, a kite flier must make sure the kite doesn't tear or spin around. The kite must catch less of the wind. The person holding the string flies the kite at a lower angle.

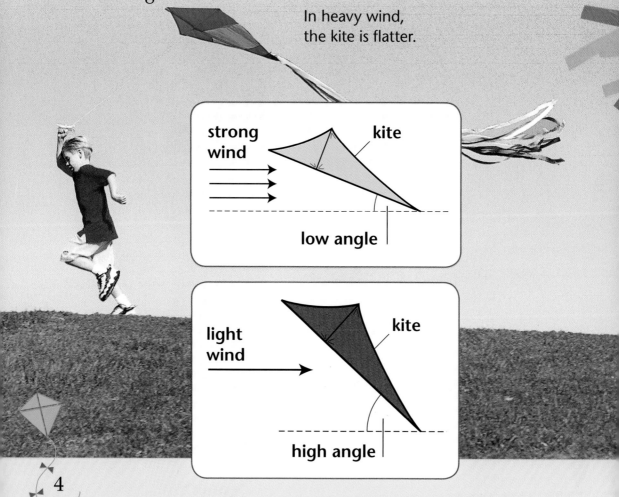

In heavy wind, the kite is flatter.

strong wind · kite · low angle

light wind · kite · high angle

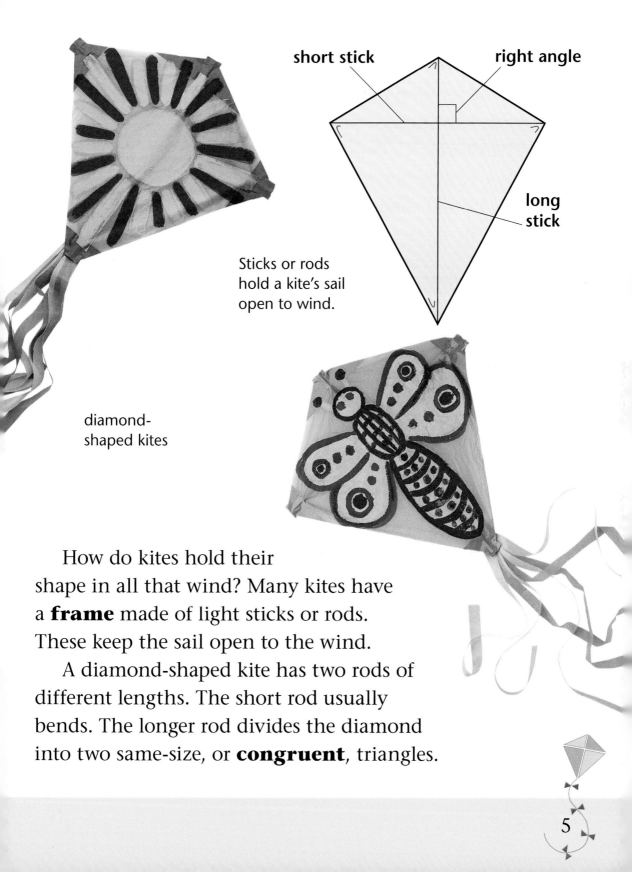

short stick

right angle

long stick

Sticks or rods hold a kite's sail open to wind.

diamond-shaped kites

How do kites hold their shape in all that wind? Many kites have a **frame** made of light sticks or rods. These keep the sail open to the wind.

A diamond-shaped kite has two rods of different lengths. The short rod usually bends. The longer rod divides the diamond into two same-size, or **congruent**, triangles.

Why is it that some kites have tails and others don't? Kites with a **bowed** shape do not need tails. The short stick bends, forming an angle between the sails. The bowed shape gives the kite different surfaces. Wind pushes the surfaces to keep the kite flying.

Kites that have just one flat surface, or **face**, need tails. The tail keeps the kite stable so it doesn't spin. The tail pulls the face of the kite in the right direction so that it catches the wind correctly.

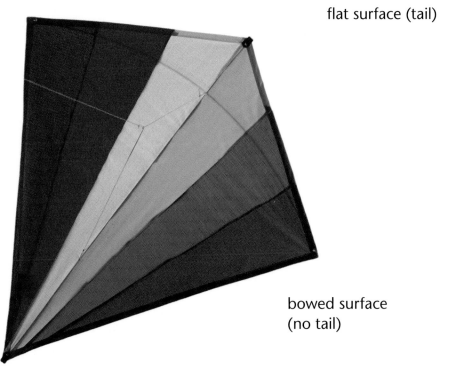

flat surface (tail)

bowed surface
(no tail)

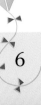

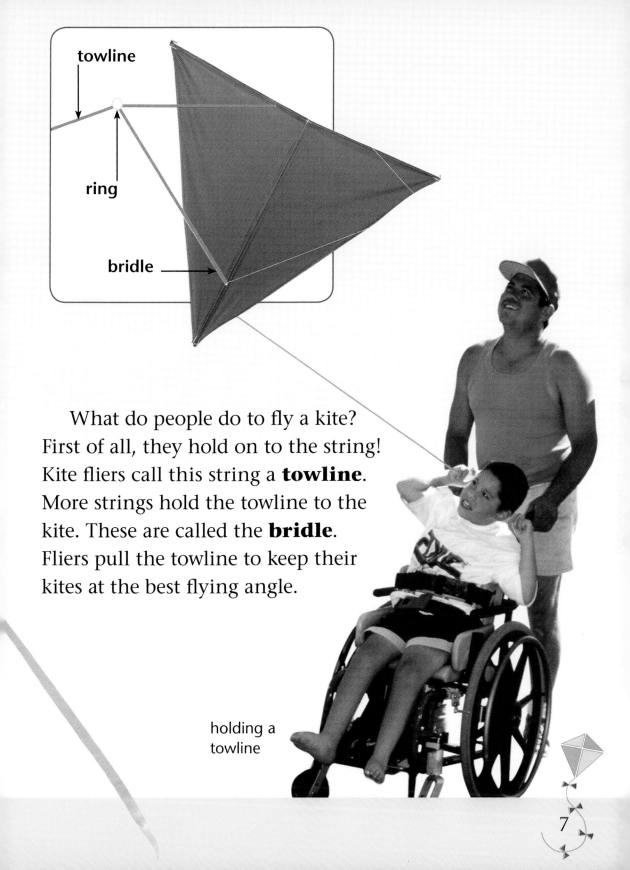

towline

ring

bridle

What do people do to fly a kite? First of all, they hold on to the string! Kite fliers call this string a **towline**. More strings hold the towline to the kite. These are called the **bridle**. Fliers pull the towline to keep their kites at the best flying angle.

holding a towline

Delta Kites

On a day with light breezes, it's fun to toss a delta kite into the wind. Delta kites are also called bat kites. The shape can look like a bat's wings.

The sail of a delta kite is usually a triangle shape. These kites often have bright patterns or pictures. They can look like birds or frogs.

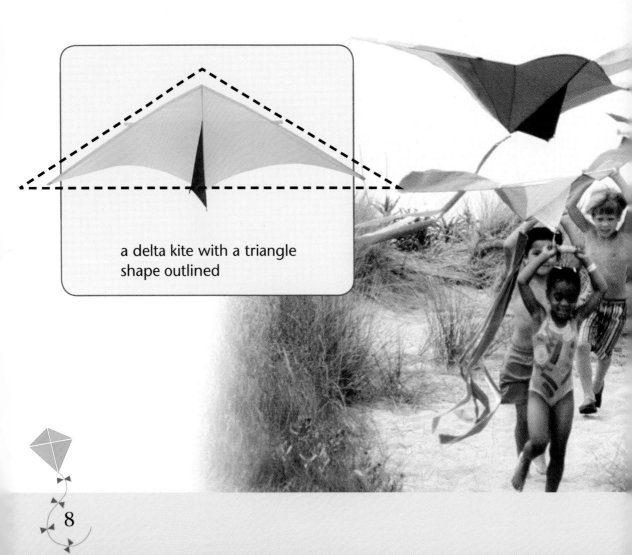

a delta kite with a triangle shape outlined

Think about what you've learned about kites so far. Does a delta kite need a tail? If you said no, you are right. Some people will add a tail to a delta kite just for fun. The kite will fly without a tail, though. It floats on the air.

The tails on these delta kites are just there to make the kites look good.

Box Kites

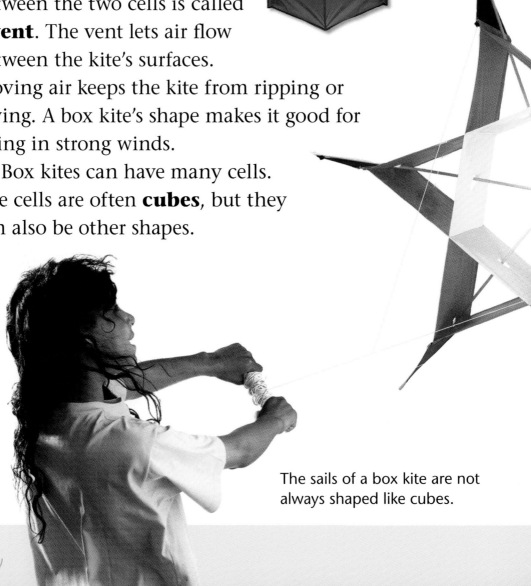

one side of the cube

vent

cell

Box kites are named for their sails. These boxlike sails are called **cells**. A simple box kite has two cells. One cell is above the other. The space between the two cells is called a **vent**. The vent lets air flow between the kite's surfaces. Moving air keeps the kite from ripping or diving. A box kite's shape makes it good for flying in strong winds.

Box kites can have many cells. The cells are often **cubes**, but they can also be other shapes.

The sails of a box kite are not always shaped like cubes.

Sled Kites

Do you like challenges? Try flying a sled kite in a strong wind. These kites can have vents, just like box kites. The frame is made from two or more sticks that hold the sails. The sticks divide the sail into three parts. A sled kite can be hard to fly. There is no cross stick to keep the sides open. Wind can make the kite collapse. People fly sled kites anyway. They are easy to make.

Fly a sled kite in light to moderate winds.

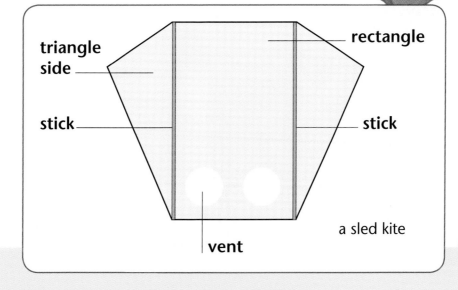

triangle side

rectangle

stick

stick

vent

a sled kite

Bell's Kites

Alexander Graham Bell invented the telephone in 1876. Bell also made huge kites of many shapes. Someone said one of his kites was as "big as a barn."

Bell made one kite with two **hexagons**. A hexagon has six sides. A center pole held the two hexagons together.

Bell's kite made
with hexagons

Bell also built a kite strong enough to lift a person 30 feet off the ground. This kite had more than 1,000 cells. Each cell had four congruent triangles. A shape with four triangle sides is called a **tetrahedron**.

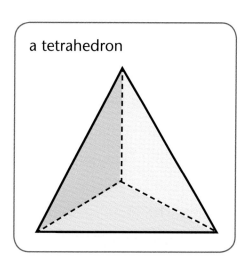

a tetrahedron

one of Bell's kites, made of tetrahedron cells

Go Fly a Kite!

Now that you know about kite shapes, what kind of kite would you choose to fly? Would you like to fly a box kite in strong winds? Perhaps you'd like to make a sled kite and try to fly it. You might choose a diamond kite with a long tail.

No matter what kind of kite you choose to fly, one thing is sure: With a kite and a string in hand, all you need to have a great time is a good breeze.

Glossary

bowed   bent or curved

bridle   strings that join the kite to the towline

cells   single units in a structure

congruent   having the same size and shape

cubes   solid figures made of six equal squares; boxes with six equal sides

face   a flat surface or side of a shape

frame   sticks or rods that keep a kite's sails open to the wind

hexagons   shapes with six straight sides

sail   paper or light fabric that covers a kite's frame

tetrahedron   a solid shape with four triangle sides

towline   string used by a kite flier to handle a kite

vent   an opening for air flow

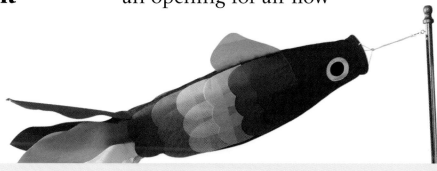

Index